The Ultimate Waitering Notebook

Name: ....

Cell: ....

Dr Carl J Davis

East London, South Africa

2020

Copyright © 2020

Dr. Carl J Davis

All rights reserved.

No portion of this publication may be duplicated without the written consent of the author.

First publication 2020

Contact: carljdavis@gmail.com

https://www.facebook.com/drcarljdavis

https://www.amazon.com/Dr-Carl-Davis/e/B00XRZ40TW

Developer: Dr. Carl J Davis

Cover page designed by Dr. Carl J Davis

Just over six years ago I was approached by the Western Cape Education Department (Adult Based Education) in the George area of the Western Cape, South Africa, to develop a course that could assist the Adult Learners with possible employment.

The decision to develop a Waitering Course was made seeing that the Western Cape has some of South Africa's most beautiful surroundings and therefore a haven for tourists.

In the same time, Golf Courses in the area also requested that I present a similar course to their restaurant staff.

This course has been presented to nearly 600 people in the just over two years, and over 2000 students since then.

In 2016 this course was also presented to 3 Star Hotels and Guest Houses in the Eastern Cape, South Africa

Get the book here - https://www.amazon.com/So-You-want-waiter-practical-waitering-ebook/dp/B01KAFR3V8/ref=sr_1_1?dchild=1&keywords=so+you+want+to+be+a+waiter&qid=1609170836&sr=8-1

I dedicate this Book to our youngest son, Brent, who has been in the Hospitality industry for 8 years.

He has shown me that, although the Industry is tough, you can still live your passion!

My Goals:

Sales and Gratuity

This Week	$
This Month	$
This Year	$

Saving Plans

This Week	$
This Month	$
This Year	$

Ultimate Goal
(The reward I am working to)

This Week	$
This Month	$
This Year	$

Hours Worked Log

WK=Week number, M,T,W,TH,FR,SA,SU = Days of the week

T=Total for the week

WK	M	T	W	TH	FR	SA	SU	T
1								
2								
3								
4								
5								
6								
7								
8								
9								
10								
11								
12								
13								
14								
15								
16								
17								
18								

WK	M	T	W	TH	FR	SA	SU	T
19								
20								
21								
22								
23								
24								
25								
26								
27								
28								
29								
30								
31								
32								
33								
34								
35								
36								
37								
38								
39								

WK	M	T	W	TH	FR	SA	SU	T
40								
42								
43								
44								
45								
46								
47								
48								
49								
50								
51								
52								
(53)								

Total hours

Hours Worked Log
(Per Month)

Month	Hours	Rate /Hour	Total
Jan			
Feb			
Mar			
Apr			
May			
Jun			
Jul			
Aug			
Sept			
Oct			
Nov			
Dec			

Average /month

Total for the Year

What will make you stand out as a SUCCESSFUL Waiter?

Hardworking – Think of the hours that you are expected to be on your feet – and then to still be polite, friendly, welcoming to serve your clientele.

Flexible – The opportunity should be ceased within the moment of the opportunity.

Honest – Not only with the finances under your control, but also regarding the goodwill you have – as well as spending your work time wisely.

Resourceful – Read up about the industry, know your products and the way and portion sizes that they are presented.

Good Listener – LISTEN to your clientele – this will eliminate wrong orders – which will cost you!

Exceptional Salesperson – Learn, practise and commit yourself to upselling and cross-selling methods – it will ultimately affect your gratuity and commission!

Be able to apply Common Sense – In EVERY situation!

Hygienic and well groomed – Wash your hands – apply deodorant, brush your teeth (and your hair), use mouthwash, wear clean and well kept clothing!

Nails should be clean and neatly trimmed.

Taking Reservations

Before you take booking, make sure you know the answers to the following type of questions:

What kind of food does our restaurant offer?

Do we cater for Halal or Kosher needs?

What type of restaurant are we?

Do we accept credit cards? Are there exclusions?

Do we charge corkage? What would the charge be?

Do we have a liquor licence?

When are we open?

Are children welcome?

Are we air conditioned?

Is there a smoking area?

Do we have car parking facilities? Is there security available?

Do we cater for functions? What is the capacity of the restaurant?

How does the client find our establishment?

Are we on social media?

Is gratuity already included in the check?

What is Up-selling?

Up-selling is a sales technique permitting to increase revenues with the same number of covers, therefore increasing a restaurant's guest check average.

Basic examples

Fast food restaurants: When a burger is ordered, you will often be asked:" do you want fries with that?" If fries are already included – "Would you like an upsize? Always offer **EXTRA** and **UPSIZE**.

Or: today's soup is Clam Soup but we also have an exquisite Lobster Soup. Our salad are also very popular.

Offer **slow moving** but highly profitable Items.

Consider kitchen stock first in – first out (**FIFO**)

Suggest aperitif or wine to go with meals. Learn the art of pairing wines with meals.

Offer the specialty of the day.

Offer second servings of items ordered.

Suggest long drinks and fresh juices

Inform guest of **food portioning** for possible adjustments with their order/s. This will eliminate guests' complaints and grow your gratuity!

Know which **orders will take longer** because of preparation time.

Examples of Upselling

Someone only orders a steak, or chicken as a main course only, you can say: **"Would you care for a light crispy spinach salad to start?"**

"What kind of margaritas do you have? We have lime flavoured margaritas, or with tamarind, strawberry, **but I would suggest you our lime Premium margarita which is our most popular margarita made with a superior tequila.**

"Can I **recommend** you a sweet wine that would perfectly match with your carrot cake, we have a delicious late harvest by the glass"

Recommend: "I think you should also get / you may also want to add....."

Consult: "I have personal experience with this, and I urge you to ..."

Question: "Have you thought about? ..." "Have you ever tried? ..." "Do you know about? ..."

Power phrases: "My experience has shown me ..."

Comfort them: "Most guests take ..." "Usually, everyone else uses ..."

Ask: "Would you care for? ..." "Would you like? ..."

Help guest selecting from the menu when necessary in a pleasant manner. Do not force guests to order.

Be specific with suggestions. Ask open-ended questions and not closed ended questions

Try suggesting the **high price items first** and if possible, lower cost item if they are of similar price. Then, come down to the next lower price. The guest should not feel that you are only suggesting high price items.

Acknowledge guest's order in a courteous manner.

Invite the Chef to come and speak to the guest and helping them in suggesting Chef's specialty.

Sell items on the menu based on **personal attention to the guest**, not high pressured sales.

How to handle a Guest's Complaint

While handling Guest Complaint in Hotel or Restaurant must remember these basic points:

Listen to guest's complaint carefully, express your enthusiasm to help. Key eye contact.

Understand the matter. Never argue or interrupt when a guest is still explaining. Wait until he/she has finished.

Analyse the matter wisely.

Apologize to the guest with good reason, then handle the request in priority if able, even if the complaint is not concerning your section.

Take action until the matter is completed.

Pass over the information to the HOD / GM / EAM immediately, if it is out of your capabilities.

Make the guest feel very comfortable while waiting and allow time for the guest to cool down.

When you see the guest at a later time, greet him and ask if everything is fine.

Log in follow up book for your colleagues to be aware of the situation.

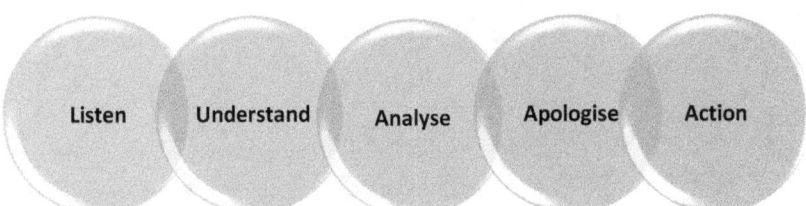

Date

Notes:

Date

Notes:

Date

Notes:

Date

Notes:

Date

Notes:

Date

Notes:

Date

Notes:

Date

Notes:

Date

Notes:

Date

Notes:

Date

Notes:

Date

Notes:

Date

Notes:

Date

Notes:

Date

Notes:

Date

Notes:

Date

Notes:

Date

Notes:

Date

Notes:

Date

Notes:

Date

Notes:

Date

Notes:

Date

Notes:

Date

Notes:

Date

Notes:

Date

Notes:

Date

Notes:

Date

Notes:

Date

Notes:

Date

Notes:

Date

Notes:

Date

Notes:

Date

Notes:

Date

Notes:

Date

Notes:

Date

Notes:

Date

Notes:

Date

Notes:

Date

Notes:

Date

Notes:

Date

Notes:

Date

Notes:

Date

Notes:

Date

Notes:

Date

Notes:

Date

Notes:

Date

Notes:

Date

Notes:

Date

Notes:

Date

Notes:

Date

Notes:

Date

Notes:

Date

Notes:

Date

Notes:

Date

Notes:

Date

Notes:

Date

Notes:

Date

Notes:

Date

Notes:

Date

Notes:

Date

Notes:

Date

Notes:

Date

Notes:

Date

Notes:

Date

Notes:

Date

Notes:

Date

Notes:

Date

Notes:

Date

Notes:

Date

Notes:

Date

Notes:

Date

Notes:

Date

Notes:

Date

Notes:

Date

Notes:

Date

Notes:

Date

Notes:

Date

Notes:

Date

Notes:

Date

Notes:

Date

Notes:

www.ingramcontent.com/pod-product-compliance
Lightning Source LLC
Chambersburg PA
CBHW070432220526
45466CB00004B/1638